SEEDS OF CHANGE
PLANTING A PATH TO PEACE

by
Jen Cullerton Johnson

illustrated by
Sonia Lynn Sadler

LEE & LOW BOOKS · NEW YORK

"Come," Wangari's mother called. She beckoned her young daughter over to a tall tree with a wide, smooth trunk and a crown of green, oval leaves.

"Feel," her mother whispered.

Wangari spread her small hands over the tree's
trunk. She smoothed her fingers over the rough bark.

"This is the *mugumo*," her mother said. "It is home
to many. It feeds many too."

She snapped off a wild fig from a low branch, and
gave it to her daughter. Wangari ate the delicious fruit,
just as geckos and elephants did. High in the tree, birds
chirped in their nests. The branches bounced with
jumping monkeys.

"Our people, the Kikuyu of Kenya, believe that our ancestors rest in the tree's shade," her mother explained.

Wangari wrapped her arms around the trunk as if hugging her great-grandmother's spirit. She promised never to cut down the tree.

Each year the mugumo grew, and so did Wangari. As the oldest girl in her family, she had many chores. Every day she fetched water, clear and sweet, from the river. In the rainy season she planted sweet potatoes, millet, and beans. When the sun shone brightly in the dry season, she shooed the chickens into the shade.

Sometimes when her brother, Nderitu, returned from school, he and Wangari played among the arrowroot plants by the stream, where thousands of eggs hatched into tadpoles and tadpoles turned into frogs. During those times, Nderitu told Wangari what he had learned in his classes. "Plants give air for people to breathe," he said. "Twenty divided by two is ten. There are seven great seas to sail."

Wangari listened as still as a tree, but her mind swirled with curiosity like the currents in the stream. Even though she knew few Kikuyu girls who could read, Wangari dreamed of going to school and learning, just like her brother.

"I must go to school," she told him.

"You will," he promised.

Nderitu talked to their parents. "Why doesn't Wangari go to school?" he asked.

Wangari's parents knew she was smart and a hard worker. Although it was unusual for a girl to be educated, they decided to send her to school. They knew she would not disappoint them. After some time to arrange for fees and supplies, Wangari's mother came to her. "You are going to school," she told her daughter.

Wangari grinned widely and hugged her mother. "Thank you!" she cried. "I will make you proud."

Wangari walked the long road to a one-room schoolhouse with walls made of mud, a floor of dirt, and a roof of tin. In time she learned to copy her letters and trace numbers. Wangari's letters soon made words, and her words made sentences. She learned how numbers could be added and subtracted, multiplied and divided. Animals and plants, she discovered, were like human beings in many ways. They needed air, water, and nourishment too.

When Wangari finished elementary school, she was eleven years old. Her mind was like a seed rooted in rich soil, ready to grow. Wangari wanted to continue her education, but to do so she would have to leave her village and move to the capital city of Nairobi. Wangari had never been farther than her valley's ridge. She was scared.

"Go," her mother said. She picked up a handful of earth and placed it gently into her daughter's hand. "Where you go, we go."

Wangari was sad to leave, but she knew that what her mother said was true. Wherever Wangari went, so went her family, her village, and her Kikuyu ways. She kissed her family and said good-bye to the mugumo tree, remembering her promise always to protect it.

Wangari's new life in the city amazed her. Skyscrapers towered above her head, not trees. People rushed through the streets like river water over stones. At school she lived with other girls like her, all trying to weave their village customs with new city ones. At night when the girls slept, Wangari dreamed of home and the sweet figs of the mugumo tree. Her dreams reminded her to honor her Kikuyu tradition of respecting all living things.

Wangari was an excellent student, and science became her favorite subject. She especially loved studying living things. Air, she learned, was made from two molecules of oxygen bonded together. Bodies were made up of cells. Leaves changed color because of photosynthesis.

As graduation neared, Wangari told her friends she wanted to become a biologist.

"Not many native women become scientists," they told her.

"I will," she said.

Wangari would have to travel halfway around the world to the United States to study biology. She had never left Kenya and had little money. But with her teachers' help, she won a scholarship to a college in Kansas.

America was very different from Kenya. In college, many of Wangari's science professors were women. From them she learned that a woman could do anything she wanted to, even if it hadn't been done before. While Wangari discovered how molecules move under a microscope lens and how cells divide in petri dishes, she also found her strength as a woman scientist.

After she graduated from college, Wangari traveled to Pennsylvania to continue her studies. Letters from home told Wangari about changes in Kenya. The people had elected a Kikuyu president, Jomo Kenyatta. Proud of her country and proud to be Kikuyu, Wangari decided to return home to Kenya to help her people.

America had changed Wangari. She had discovered a spirit of possibility and freedom that she wanted to share with Kenyan women. She accepted a teaching job at the University of Nairobi. Not many women were professors then, and even fewer taught science. Wangari led the way for other women and girls. She worked for equal rights so that female scientists would be treated with the same respect as male scientists.

Wangari watched sadly as her government sold more and more land to big foreign companies that cut down forests for timber and to clear land for coffee plantations. Native trees such as cedar and acacia vanished. Without trees, birds had no place to nest. Monkeys lost their swings. Tired mothers walked miles for firewood.

When Wangari visited her village she saw that the Kikuyu custom of not chopping down the mugumo trees had been lost. No longer held in place by tree roots, the soil streamed into the rivers. The water that had been used to grow maize, bananas, and sweet potatoes turned to mud and dried up. Many families went hungry.

Wangari could not bear to think of the land being destroyed. Now married and the mother of three children, she worried about what would happen to all the mothers and children who depended on the land.

"We must do something," Wangari said.

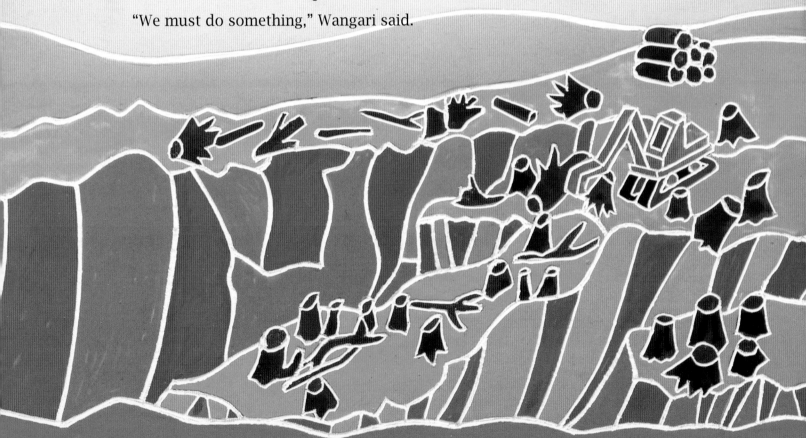

Wangari had an idea as small as a seed but as tall as a tree that reaches for the sky. "*Harabee!* Let's work together!" she said to her countrywomen—mothers like her. Wangari dug deep into the soil, a seedling by her side. "We must plant trees."

Many women listened. Many planted seedlings. Some men laughed and sneered. Planting trees was women's work, they said. Others complained that Wangari was too outspoken—with too many opinions and too much education for a woman.

Wangari refused to listen to those who criticized her.

Instead she told them, "Those trees [you] are cutting down today were not planted by [you] but by those who came before. You must plant trees that will benefit the community to come, like a seedling with sun, good soil, and abundant rain, the roots of our future will bury themselves in the ground and a canopy of hope will reach the sky."

Wangari traveled to villages, towns, and cities with saplings and seeds, shovels and hoes. At each place she went, women planted rows of trees that looked like green belts across the land. Because of this they started calling themselves the Green Belt Movement.

"We might not change the big world but we can change the landscape of the forest," she said.

One tree turned to ten, ten to one hundred, one hundred to one
million, all the way up to thirty million planted trees. Kenya grew green
again. Birds nested in new trees. Monkeys swung on branches. Rivers
filled with clean water. Wild figs grew heavy in mugumo branches.

Mothers fed their children maize, bananas, and sweet potatoes until they could eat no more.

As the Green Belts moved farther across Kenya, powerful voices rose up against Wangari's movement. Foreign business people, greedy for more land for their coffee plantations and trees for timber, asked, "Who is this woman who can change so many lives with a sapling? Why should we give up our land and profits for trees?"

They made a plan to stop Wangari.

One day while she was out planting a tree, some wealthy businessmen paid corrupt police officers to arrest Wangari.

In her jail cell, Wangari prayed. And like a sturdy tree against a mighty wind, her faith kept her strong. Instead of giving up, she made friends with the other women prisoners. They told her their stories. She taught them about her seeds and saplings. Together, they helped one another.

Wangari knew many people in Kenya and other countries. They banded together to fight for her release. Before she was freed, Wangari promised to help fight for the rights of the other women prisoners too.

Wangari realized that the people who had put her in jail didn't like the changes in the land or in the women. The people in charge of big companies wanted to keep the land for themselves, and the government was frightened of too many advances made by women. If she wanted to help save her country and countrywomen, Wangari would have to go out into the world to spread her message. She would have to leave her home once more.

Wangari began to travel, telling her story to teachers, presidents, farmers, ambassadors, and schoolchildren all over the world. She dug in the dirt, planted seedlings, and spoke about women's rights. With everyone she met, she shared the seeds of change.

In time Kenya changed. More people listened to Wangari's message, calling her the *Mama Miti*, "Mother of Trees." They wanted her to lead them into Kenya's new democracy. Wangari was elected to Kenya's parliament and became minister of the environment.

Still, she did not stop planting trees.

In 2004 Wangari won the most prestigious peace prize in the world, the Nobel Peace Prize. It had never before been awarded to an African woman or an environmentalist.

Standing in front of an audience of people from around the world, far from her village, Wangari remembered her girlhood lesson of the mugumo. She understood that persistence, patience, and commitment—to an idea as small as a seed but as tall as a tree that reaches for the sky—must be planted in every child's heart. "Young people, you are our hope and our future," she said.

And then, as she had done so many times before, Wangari planted a tree.

Wangari Maathai won the Nobel Peace Prize in 2004 at the age of sixty-four. Today she is still active, planting trees and promoting the rights of women and children. She lives in Kenya with memories of her mother's teaching about the mugumo. The Green Belt Movement that Wangari founded in 1977 has spread around the world, teaching people to take care of the environment by planting trees, recycling, and seeking alternative energy sources. Wangari says, "Through the Green Belt Movement we have helped young people get involved in environmental activities. We have tried to instill in them the idea that protecting the environment is not just a pleasure but also a duty."

To Cecelia, my grandmother, and all my
students, may you take root and flourish.
—J.C.J.

To my mother, Inez Sadler, and my family,
who have supported me unconditionally in
my efforts, since childhood, as an artist.
—S.L.S.

Author's Sources

Maathai, Wangari. *The Green Belt Movement:*
  Sharing the Approach and the Experience.
  New York: Lantern Books, 2003, revised 2006.
——. *Unbowed: A Memoir.* New York: Alfred A. Knopf, 2006.

Quotation Sources

p. 10: "Why . . . school?" *Unbowed: A Memoir* by Wangari
  Maathai, p. 40.
p. 24: "Those trees . . . the sky." Ibid., p. 289.
p. 39: "persistence, patience, and commitment" Ibid.

Adapted from the transcript of Wangari Maathai's Nobel Lecture:
http://nobelprize.org/nobel_prizes/peace/laureates/2004/
maathai-lecture-text.html
p. 39: "Young people . . . you are our hope and our future."

Text copyright © 2010 by Jen Cullerton Johnson
Illustrations copyright © 2010 by Sonia Lynn Sadler

Manufactured in China by Jade Productions, June 2016

Book design by Scott Myles Studios
Book production by The Kids at Our House

The text is set in Lucida Bright
The illustrations are rendered in scratchboard and oil

15 14 13 12 11 10
First Edition

Library of Congress Cataloging-in-Publication Data
Johnson, Jen Cullerton.
Seeds of change : Planting a path to peace / by Jen Cullerton
Johnson ; illustrated by Sonia Lynn Sadler. — 1st ed.
        p. cm.
    Summary: "A biography of Kenyan Nobel Peace Prize winner
and environmentalist Wangari Maathai, a female scientist who
made a stand in the face of opposition to women's rights and
her own Green Belt Movement, an effort to restore Kenya's
ecosystem by planting millions of trees"—Provided by publisher.
    ISBN 978-1-60060-367-9 (hardcover : alk. paper)
1. Maathai, Wangari—Juvenile literature. 2. Tree planters
(Persons)—Kenya—Biography—Juvenile literature. 3. Green
Belt Movement (Society : Kenya)—Juvenile literature. 4. Women
conservationists—Kenya—Biography—Juvenile literature.
5. Women politicians—Kenya—Biography—Juvenile literature.
6. Women's rights—Kenya—Juvenile literature. 7. Nobel Prize
winners—Biography—Juvenile literature. 8. Women Nobel
Prize winners—Biography—Juvenile literature. 9. Kenya—
Environmental conditions—Juvenile literature. 10. Kenya—
Biography—Juvenile literature. I. Sadler, Sonia Lynn, ill.
II. Title.
SB63.M22J646 20010
333.72092—dc22
[B]   2009043239